TOP TEN COUNTRIES OF RECENT IMMIGRANTS

CHINA

A MYREPORTLINKS.COM BOOK

KIM A. O'CONNELL

MyReportLinks.com Books

an imprint of

Enslow Publishers, Inc.

E

Box 398, 40 Industrial Road
Berkeley Heights, NJ 07922
USA

MyReportLinks.com Books, an imprint of Enslow Publishers, Inc. MyReportLinks®
is a registered trademark of Enslow Publishers, Inc.

Library of Congress Cataloging-in-Publication Data

O'Connell, Kim A.
  China / Kim A. O'Connell.
     p. cm. — (Top ten countries of recent immigrants)
  Includes bibliographical references and index.
   ISBN 0-7660-5240-0
   1. China—Juvenile literature. [1. China. 2. Chinese Americans.] I.
Title. II. Series.
   DS706.O296 2004
   951—dc22

                              2003022662

Printed in the United States of America

10 9 8 7 6 5 4 3 2 1

To Our Readers:
Through the purchase of this book, you and your library gain access to the Report Links that specifically back
up this book.
The Publisher will provide access to the Report Links that back up this book and will keep these Report Links
up to date on **www.myreportlinks.com** for three years from the book's first publication date.
We have done our best to make sure all Internet addresses in this book were active and appropriate when we
went to press. However, the author and the Publisher have no control over, and assume no liability for, the
material available on those Internet sites or on other Web sites they may link to.
The usage of the MyReportLinks.com Books Web site is subject to the terms and conditions stated on the
Usage Policy Statement on **www.myreportlinks.com**.
A password may be required to access the Report Links that back up this book. The password is found on the
bottom of page 4 of this book.
Any comments or suggestions can be sent by e-mail to comments@myreportlinks.com or to the address on
the back cover.

Contents

CHINA

Report Links **4**

China Facts **9**

1 **An Ancient Heritage** **10**

2 **A Staircase With Three Steps:
     Land and Climate** **14**

3 **Yin and Yang: Culture** **19**

4 **Embracing the Future: Economy** **25**

5 **Confucius to Communism: History** **29**

6 **The "Golden Mountain":
     Chinese Americans** **40**

Chapter Notes **46**

Further Reading **47**

Index **48**

MyReportLinks.com Books
Great Books, Great Links, Great for Research!

The Report Links listed on the following four pages can save you hours of research time by **instantly** bringing you to the best Web sites relating to your report topic.

How to Use MyReportLinks.com

1. Got a Report to do?

2. Check out a MyReportLinks.com Book at the Library.

3. Read the Book.

4. Go to www.myreportlinks.com for Quick, Safe, and Up-to-Date Links!

5. Internet Report Links = Great Information.

6. Write Your Report. Impress Your Teacher.

MAX LYNX

The pre-evaluated Web sites are your links to source documents, photographs, illustrations, and maps. They also provide links to dozens—even hundreds—of Web sites about your report subject.

MyReportLinks.com Books and the MyReportLinks.com Web site save you time and make report writing easier than ever!

Please see "To Our Readers" on the copyright page for important information about this book, the MyReportLinks.com Web site, and the Report Links that back up this book. Please enter **ICH5890** if asked for a password.

Report Links

The Internet sites described below can be accessed at
http://www.myreportlinks.com

*EDITOR'S CHOICE

▶The *World Factbook*: China

This page from the *World Factbook* contains statistics about China. Geography, people, government, economy, communications, transportation, the military, and transnational issues are covered here.

*EDITOR'S CHOICE

▶Becoming American: The Chinese Experience

This multimedia PBS site explores what life in America is like for some Chinese Americans. Documentary clips, an interactive time line, and Chinese family portraits are some of the features.

*EDITOR'S CHOICE

▶Great Wall of China

The construction of the Great Wall of China, the history of the wall, and other interesting facts about this amazing structure are featured in this site.

*EDITOR'S CHOICE

▶China—A Country Study

This Library of Congress site contains a comprehensive study of China. Information about geography, culture, history, government, economics, religion, language, and many other subjects can be found here.

*EDITOR'S CHOICE

▶Tiananmen Revisited

In the summer of 1989, students protesting abuses of the Chinese government were attacked and some killed in Beijing's Tiananmen Square. This CNN site offers a retrospective of the events that took place and what has changed, and not changed, in Chinese policy since.

*EDITOR'S CHOICE

▶American Memory: Chinese Immigration

This Library of Congress American Memory site tells the story of early Chinese immigration to the United States. Inside you will find information about Chinese labor, anti-Chinese racism and legislation, and Chinese communities in the United States.

The Internet sites described below can be accessed at
http://www.myreportlinks.com

▶**Amy Tan: Best-Selling Novelist**

Amy Tan, whose parents emigrated from China to California, is one of the most popular contemporary authors in the United States. Here you will find a brief biography of the author as well as an interview with her.

▶**China**

This site from the United Nations Cyberschoolbus site provides a basic overview of China, including information on China's economy, environment, healthcare, technology, and more.

▶**China Knowledge: A Universal Guide for China Studies**

This comprehensive site contains a wealth of information about Chinese culture. Inside you will find in-depth explanations of Chinese history, arts, music, writing, language, philosophy, religion, and literature.

▶**China the Beautiful**

China the Beautiful offers a wide variety of resources related to Chinese culture. Here you can learn Chinese, listen to a recording of the Beijing Opera, view calligraphy samples, and much more.

▶**China's Christian Warrior**

This *TimeAsia* site offers a brief biography of Chiang Kai-shek, who tried to unify a divided China. He was ultimately forced to flee to the island of Taiwan, where he set up a separate government.

▶**Chinavoc.com**

Chinavoc.com is a Chinese web site dedicated to various aspects of Chinese culture. History, festivals, arts, and kung fu are the most comprehensive sections.

▶**Chinese Exclusion Act**

The Chinese Exclusion Act of 1882 prohibited Chinese immigrants from entering the United States. Here you will find the complete document, its 1904 extension, and its 1943 repeal.

▶**Chinese-American Contributions to Transcontinental Railroad**

This page from the Central Pacific Railroad Photographic History Museum contains a wealth of information, photographs, and links related to the Chinese-American laborers who built the railroad.

Report Links

The Internet sites described below can be accessed at http://www.myreportlinks.com

▶ **Chung, Connie: U.S. Broadcast Journalist**

This Museum of Broadcast Communication site casts the spotlight on Connie Chung, a broadcast journalist with a long and distinguished career.

▶ **CNN.com: Visions of China**

This in-depth CNN site commemorates the People's Republic of China in its fiftieth year. Inside you will learn about China's politics, economics, people, and provinces.

▶ **Country Profile: China**

This BBC portrait of China contains information about Chinese politics, history, economics, and more. You can also listen to China's national anthem when you visit the site.

▶ **Cultural Ambassadors: Yo-Yo Ma**

The world-renowned cellist Yo-Yo Ma is profiled in this site. Here you will get a brief overview of the man and his music.

▶ **Dreams of Tibet: A Troubled Country and Its Enduring Fascination**

This PBS Frontline site examines issues regarding Tibet. Tibetan Buddhism and China's relationship with Tibet are discussed at length.

▶ **History of China**

This site provides an overview of Chinese history from prehistoric times to the Qing dynasty, China's last dynasty, which was overthrown in 1911.

▶ **Mao Tse-Tung**

This CNN site offers a brief overview of Mao Tse-Tung (or Mao Zedong), the Communist leader of China whose influence was felt in that nation for more than forty years.

▶ **Museum of Qin Terra-Cotta Warriors and Horses**

This site offers a look inside the Museum of the Qin Terra-cotta Warriors and Horses, in Shaanxi province, which features thousands of life-size figures found near the tomb of an ancient emperor.

Report Links

The Internet sites described below can be accessed at http://www.myreportlinks.com

▶**Selected Chinese Myths and Fantasies**

China's long history has spawned many interesting myths and legends. Some of the best-known can be read by clicking on the links at this site.

▶**Separate Lives, Broken Dreams**

This site explores the impact that Chinese exclusion legislation had on the lives of people in America and China. Here you will find immigration documents, legislation, and other resources.

▶**Six Billion and Beyond: China**

More people live in China than in any other country in the world. This PBS site contains information about factors related to China's population and what is being done to control it.

▶**State of Washington: Governor Gary Locke**

Gary Locke, governor of Washington State, is the nation's first Chinese-American governor. Here you will find information about his life, work, and political beliefs.

▶***Time* 100: Mao Zedong**

Mao Zedong (also spelled Mao Tse-Tung) was the first leader of the People's Republic of China. A brief biography and time line are included in this site.

▶**To Have and Have Not**

China joined the World Trade Organization in 2001. This PBS site examines the consequences that China's membership in this organization will have on worldwide trade and also on the United States economy.

▶**US Figure Skating Online: Michelle Kwan**

Michelle Kwan, a world-champion figure skater, is one of the most popular skaters of recent times. Here you will learn about her many achievements.

▶**The *World Factbook*: Taiwan**

This page from the *World Factbook* contains statistics about Taiwan. Geography, people, government, economy, communications, transportation, military, and transnational issues are covered here.

China Facts

▶ **Capital**
Beijing

▶ **Population**
1,286,975,468[1]

▶ **Land Area**
3,705,386 square miles
(9,595,960 square kilometers); world's fourth-largest
country, after Russia, Canada,
and the United States.[2]

▶ **Type of Government**
Communist state

▶ **Location**
Eastern Asia

▶ **Highest Point**
Mount Everest (bordering
Tibet and Nepal), the world's
highest peak at 29,035 feet
(8,850 meters)

▶ **Lowest Point**
Turpan Pendi, 505 feet
(154 meters) below sea level

▶ **Ethnic Groups**
Han Chinese 91.9%,
Zhuang, Uygur, Hui, Yi,
Tibetan, Miao, Manchu,
Mongol, Buyi, Korean, and
other nationalities, 8.1%

▶ **Religions**
Daoist (Taoist), Buddhist,
Muslim 1% to 2%, Christian
3% to 4%. The state is
officially atheist.

▶ **Literacy Rate**
86% overall

▶ **Languages**
Standard Chinese or Mandarin
(Putonghua, based on the
Beijing dialect),
Yue (Cantonese),
Wu (Shanghaiese), and other
minority languages

▶ **National Holiday**
October 1 is celebrated as the
Anniversary of the Founding
of the People's Republic of
China (1949).

▶ **Flag**
The flag of the People's
Republic of China features a
red field with a large yellow star
in the upper left corner; four
smaller yellow five-pointed
stars arranged in a vertical arc
are to the right of the large star.

An Ancient Heritage

Imagine a structure so large that it took not years, not even decades, but centuries to build. Imagine that construction began in ancient times and continued, in one form or another, until the middle of the twentieth century. It may sound impossible, but it is the story of the Great Wall of China, the largest structure ever built. The wall zigzags across and over China's mountainous landscape for more than eighteen hundred miles. Begun in the third century B.C. to keep out invaders, the wall is actually more like a long castle, complete with lookout towers. Sections of the Great Wall have been joined and rebuilt over the course of many centuries since. In the middle of the twentieth century, for example, two sections of the wall were reconstructed and opened to tourists.

The Great Wall seems like the perfect symbol for China, whose history is also long and full of twists and turns. China, which has the world's oldest continuing civilization, has a history that dates back about four thousand years. This large nation has witnessed powerful dynasties, brutal wars, and strong leaders. Today, China is the world's most populous nation, with about 1.29 billion people.

▷ Places to Visit

In addition to the Great Wall, China has many natural and historic sites for tourists to visit. Major cities such as Beijing, Shanghai, and Hong Kong offer visitors abundant opportunities to experience Chinese culture. For example,

Beijing, China's capital, contains the magnificent Palace Museum, formerly known as the Forbidden City, a complex of architectural wonders that is completely surrounded by a continuous wall. Halls, terraces, and gateways showcase marble figures, glazed terra-cotta, tiles, and ornate woodwork. The best-known gate is called Tiananmen, or the Gate of Heavenly Peace, which overlooks the famous square of the same name. Also in Beijing is the large Temple of Heaven, a massive round structure topped with a three-tiered roof, which was visited by Chinese emperors to honor Heaven and perform certain rituals.

Tiananmen Square's history is marked by both triumph and tragedy. The square contains several important Chinese monuments, the museum of history, and the Mao Zedong (Mao Tse-Tung) Memorial Hall. The first leader of Communist China, Mao proclaimed the founding of the People's Republic of China from the rostrum on top

▲ The Terra-cotta Warriors and Horses are considered by many to be the eighth wonder of the world.

of Tiananmen on October 1, 1949. This anniversary is still observed there. But Tiananmen Square was also the scene of a large demonstration that took place forty years later. In June 1989, Chinese students staged a massive pro-democracy rally there. The Chinese army responded with tanks and weapons and it is believed that hundreds were killed, although the Chinese government has never released an official figure.

China contains many other sites that are covered in mystery. One such site is the Terra-cotta Warriors Museum in the city of Xi'an, in Shaanxi Province. The museum contains more than six thousand life-size terra-cotta figures that were discovered through archaeological excavations of the tomb of Emperor Qin Shi Huangdi.

The Yellow Mountains are one of China's most popular natural wonders. With their peaks often surrounded by fog and mist, these rocky mountains form strange and beautiful shapes. Steep mountain trails are often crowded with tourists, who can relax in nearby hot springs after a day of hiking.

Famous Chinese Americans

Although China is home to more people than any other nation, millions of Chinese have also emigrated from China to the United States and other countries. Chinese Americans have become well known in many fields. Famous Chinese immigrants and Chinese Americans include architect I. M. Pei, who designed the pyramid at the Louvre Museum in Paris, and architect Maya Lin, who designed the Vietnam Veterans Memorial in Washington, D.C. Writers Amy Tan and Maxine Hong Kingston have dealt with the differences between American and Chinese cultures. Figure skater Michelle

State of
Washington

Our Governor

GOVERNOR GARY LOCKE'S BIOGRAPHY

ary Locke was elected Washington's 21st governor on Nov. 5, 1996, aking him the first Chinese-American governor in U.S. history. On Nov. 7, 2000, Locke, a Democrat, was re-elected to his second term. As governor, he has worked to make Washington a better place to live, work and raise a family by:

Making our schools the best in the nation.

Strengthening our state's economy with an efficient, effective transportation system and business climate.

Making state government more accessible and user-friendly while ensuring it delivers to taxpayers the services they most need at a reasonable and sustainable cost.

orn into an immigrant family on Jan. 21, 1950, Locke spent his first six ears in Seattle's Yesler Terrace, a public housing project for families of World War II veterans. He worked in his father's grocery store, became an

Meet the First Lady

Mona Locke, wife of Washington Governor Gary Locke, became the state's twentieth First Lady on January 15, 1997.

The Locke Family

The Governor's family has a long history in Washington. His grandfather came to the Evergreen State at the turn of the century.

The Governor's Mansion

To go on a virtual tour of the mansion, select the photo of the Executive Mansion

 🐾 Internet

▲ *In 1996, Governor Gary Locke of Washington State became the first Chinese-American governor in American history.*

Kwan, whose parents emigrated from China in the 1970s, is a world champion and Olympic medalist.

When he was inaugurated as governor of Washington in 1997, Gary Locke became the first Chinese-American governor in the history of the United States. In a 2003 speech, Locke talked about the importance of celebrating Chinese culture.

I am proud to be an American, and I am proud of my Chinese ancestry and cultural heritage. I am proud of the enormous contributions China has made to civilization over the past thousands of years, and will continue to make in the future.[1]

A Staircase With Three Steps: Land and Climate

The centerpiece of eastern Asia, China is the world's fourth-largest country in terms of land area behind Russia, Canada, and the United States. It is bordered by many countries, including Mongolia, Russia, and Kazakhstan to the north, North Korea to the east, Vietnam, India, and Nepal to the south, and Pakistan and Afghanistan to the west.

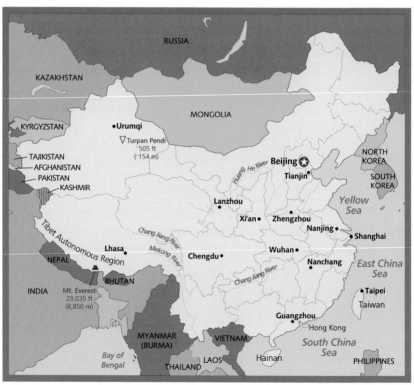

▲ A map of China.

With a landscape that ranges from mountains to coastal plains, China's climate varies greatly. The northern parts of China experience freezing winter temperatures as low as −40°F and hot summers that reach as high as 100°F. Central China's seasons are somewhat less extreme. In southeastern China, the climate is more tropical, with hot, humid summers that sometimes bring typhoons, massive storms with high winds and heavy rains that occur in the lands that border the China Sea.

▶ Land and Water

China's landscape is sometimes called the "staircase with three steps," descending from west to east. Western China is the site of the country's highest points, including the soaring mountains of the Himalayas. Mount Everest, the world's tallest mountain at 29,035 feet, sits on the border of Tibet (which China claims as an autonomous region) and Nepal. Central China steps down to smaller mountains and foothills. Eastern China contains the lowest "step," the coastal plains.

Cutting through this dramatic landscape are several major rivers. The longest of these is the 2,432-mile (6,300-km) Yangzi (Yangtze) River, also known as the Chang Jiang ("Long River"), the third-longest river in the world after the Nile in Africa and the Amazon in South America.[1] The farmland around the Yangzi River is so fertile that the region is often called the "rice bowl of China." The Huang He or Yellow River is another major waterway, flowing eastward for about three thousand miles. The river was named for the yellowish silt it carries along and deposits around its mouth.

One of China's most remarkable waterways was made by humans. China's Grand Canal extends for about one

▲ *Tiananmen Square in Beijing has been the scene of both triumph and tragedy in China's history.*

thousand miles from Beijing to Hangzhou, forming an important north-south waterway in eastern China. Construction on the canal began in the sixth century B.C. and continued for more than two thousand years. Although roads and railroads replaced the canal as the primary ways to move goods, many portions are still in heavy use.

China also has an extremely long coastline that stretches for nearly nine thousand miles along three bodies of water: the Yellow, East China, and South China seas.

▷ Major Cities

In contrast to China's rugged, remote regions, its largest cities are busy, crowded, and always changing. Located in northeast China, Beijing, the nation's capital, is a complex mix of old and new. In the shadow of monuments to China's past, such as the Palace Museum and Tiananmen

Square, Beijing's citizens bike, take buses or trolleys, or ride motor scooters through crowded streets to get to work. Beijing is home to modern office towers, hotels, universities, and shopping and entertainment districts.

Although Beijing is bustling, Shanghai is actually China's largest city. Located on China's eastern coastline, at the mouth of the Yangzi River, Shanghai is a thriving cultural and financial center. The city boasts an opera house and a museum that features an extensive collection of ancient and modern Chinese art.

Hong Kong, which is located on an island and surrounding mainland areas in southeast China, is one of China's most interesting cities. Since Hong Kong was a British crown colony for more than a century, it is still home to sizable British, American, and Indian populations in addition to Chinese. In 1997, China regained sovereignty of Hong Kong, which is now considered a special administrative region. Hong Kong is also a major trading and financial center.

▶ Taiwan and Tibet

China is divided into twenty-three provinces, including the disputed territories of Taiwan and

There are fewer than one ▶ thousand giant pandas in existence, and those not in zoos live in several regions of China. Although pandas exist mainly on bamboo, they also eat flowers, vines, honey, and rodents.

Tibet. Taiwan is a large island off the east coast of China. After the Communists came to power, many members of China's Nationalist party fled to Taiwan and eventually set up a democratic government there. Ever since, Communist Chinese and Taiwanese leaders have argued over which government should rule Taiwan. Some say that Taiwan should be unified with Communist China, but others say that Taiwan's independence should be recognized.

Tibet is almost the geographical opposite of Taiwan. Whereas Taiwan is a semitropical island, Tibet is located high in the snowcapped Himalayan and Kunlun mountain ranges—known to the local people as the "Land of Snow." Like Taiwan, however, Tibet is a disputed territory. In the 1950s, the Chinese government seized control of Tibet. In the process, Chinese leaders destroyed aspects of ancient Tibetan culture, such as Buddhist monasteries. Historically, Tibet was led by Buddhist monks, with the highest position held by the Dalai Lama. The present Dalai Lama, who lives in exile in northern India, is still a respected religious leader. In recent years, people all over the world have protested that Tibet should be freed from Chinese rule.

Yin and Yang: Culture

In Chinese thought, dual forces are always at work in the universe, balancing each other out. This is the guiding principle of "yin and yang." The opposing forces of yin and yang are usually expressed by a round black-and-white symbol, with yin suggestive of the light and female side and yang symbolizing the shade and the male side. This idea of harmony and balance runs through much of Chinese culture.

▶ Education

Beginning in the 1960s, Communist Chairman Mao Zedong began a program called the Cultural Revolution. Mao was suspicious of teachers and other educated people, so he closed many schools and encouraged young people to join instead the Red Guard units, made up of militant students who supported Mao's bias against free thought and liberal education. In recent years, however, the Chinese government has renewed its support for education. Major cities such as Beijing and Shanghai have several universities and other schools. Most children receive a minimum of nine years of instruction, from elementary through high school. After that point, students can attend either a vocational school, where they learn trades, or a university, where they study art and science.

▷ Religion and Philosophy

Like education, religion is central to Chinese culture although the government is officially atheist (it professes no belief in a higher power). The three most common religions in China are Buddhism, Islam, and Christianity. Buddhism, which had its beginnings in India in the sixth century B.C., is based on the teachings of Siddhartha Gautama, who became known as the Buddha. Buddhism may be the religion most closely associated with Chinese culture, although it is not a religion that is based on a belief in a supreme being. Simply put, Buddhism is based on four noble truths: that suffering exists, it has a cause, it has an end, and there is a path that leads to that end. The idea of karma, that one's actions in a past life determine the form in which one is reborn, is also central to Buddhist belief and encourages followers to think about the consequences of their behaviors.

Modern Chinese also continue to be influenced by the ancient philosophies of Confucianism and Taoism. Confucius, who

◁ *This Tibetan Buddhist monk is pictured at a monastery in Lhasa, the capital of the Tibet Autonomous Region.*

also lived in the sixth century B.C., taught that humans' destiny was beyond their control and dictated one's condition in life. His teachings influenced the Chinese tradition of obedience and respect for parents and elders. Taoism, begun by the philospher Lao Zi, calls for people to live in a natural harmony with the Tao, which is a cosmic unity that believers feel underlies all things. Taoism urges people to reject material goods and status symbols to lead a more pure and simple life in a natural state.

Festivals

The modern Chinese use two calendars. One is the calendar, used in the United States and most of the rest of the world, that begins on January 1. But the traditional Chinese calendar is a lunar calendar, based on the cycles of the moon. As a result, the Chinese New Year does not fall on the same date each year. It usually falls sometime between late January and late February. This celebration, also called the Spring Festival, often involves a parade. Sometimes, several people will line up to carry a large costume animal down the street during the celebration.

The Dragon Festival is another popular event in China. On the fifth day of the fifth lunar month, groups of paddlers decorate their canoes as dragons and race them in China's rural rivers. Dragon boat races are also popular in China's cities. As the year moves into autumn, Chinese people look forward to the Moon Festival, which falls on the autumnal equinox. The round "moon cake" is the traditional food of this festival.

Literature and the Arts

Literature and art have been thriving in China for thousands of years. The Chinese language is based on characters, not

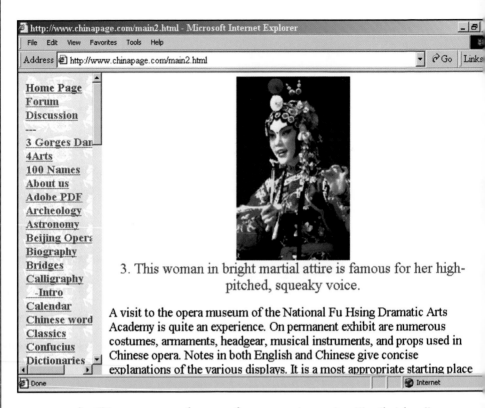

3. This woman in bright martial attire is famous for her high-pitched, squeaky voice.

A visit to the opera museum of the National Fu Hsing Dramatic Arts Academy is quite an experience. On permanent exhibit are numerous costumes, armaments, headgear, musical instruments, and props used in Chinese opera. Notes in both English and Chinese give concise explanations of the various displays. It is a most appropriate starting place

▲ *Chinese opera performers often appear in ornate attire that has its roots in the martial arts.*

letters. These characters, which represent whole words or ideas, form interesting shapes. Recognizing their beauty, Chinese artists have long painted or drawn characters in a creative way, an art form called calligraphy. Chinese paintings are similarly simple and elegant, often created with just a few brush strokes.

In the performing arts, opera and live music are popular. Chinese opera is very different from the European styles of opera known to most Americans. In China, the opera might include singing, music, acting, and even martial arts.

Another fascinating art form in China is shadow puppetry, which is similar to making shapes with one's hands in front of a light to cast shadows on the wall. Chinese shadow puppetry is far more complex, combining several Chinese art forms including sculpture, painting, drama, and literature.

Like the country's other art forms, Chinese architecture has a long and interesting tradition. Although it is hard to summarize traditional Chinese architecture, major Chinese buildings often have tiered roofs, overhanging and upturned eaves, and steep staircases. Whether designing and furnishing a major building or a small house, Chinese builders often follow the concept of feng shui. Feng shui is the practice of arranging structures or objects in a way that is believed to promote harmony and balance. In recent years, feng shui has grown popular throughout the Western world.

Sports and Games

Sports and games are popular in China. In particular, martial arts such as kung fu are practiced regularly. Tai chi, an ancient Chinese art that combines meditation and exercise, is also very popular. In many parks or open spaces in Chinese cities, groups of people practicing tai chi can be seen daily. Tai chi features slow, continuous movements that encourage deep breathing and focus. It is a form of exercise that people of all ages can take part in.

China has developed many games, including Chinese chess and mah-jongg. Today, both games are played worldwide, even through the Internet. Not to be confused with Chinese checkers, the popular Western board game, Chinese chess (also known as xiangqi) is a challenging game that may have first been played in ancient times. Mah-jongg is also complicated, involving tiles made of

Amy Tan and her mother Daisy, at home in San Francisco.

(PEOPLE Weekly © 1989 Jim McHugh)

BACK

▲ Amy Tan, an accomplished Chinese-American novelist, is seen here in San Francisco with her mother. Tan's novels lend voice to the experiences of Chinese Americans.

ivory or bone. Like playing cards, the mah-jongg tiles come in different suits. Instead of kings and queens, however, mah-jongg tiles feature dragons, bamboo, or other Chinese images.

In Amy Tan's popular novel *The Joy Luck Club*, a Chinese-American woman is asked to play mah-jongg with her mother's Chinese friends. As she moves the tiles, she listens to the women tell stories about their life in China. In the end, she visits China herself. "And now," she says, "I also see what part of me is Chinese. It is so obvious. It is my family. It is in our blood."[1]

Chapter 4 ▶

Embracing the Future: Economy

Most of China's rugged landscape is impossible to farm. Yet that has not stopped the Chinese people from finding ways to get as much out of the land as possible. More than a thousand years ago, Chinese farmers invented a crop irrigation system, using machines that pulled water buckets from nearby streams and rivers. They also began carving stepped terraces into hillsides, to provide more flat surfaces for growing rice and other crops, a method that is still used today.

About half of China's population make their living by farming and fishing. China's primary crops are rice, barley, and wheat, although other crops such as sweet potatoes, peanuts, tea, and corn are grown as well. The most common livestock are sheep, cattle, and goats, which are suited to grazing in the more mountainous regions of the country, as well as chickens and ducks.

In the 1970s, the Chinese government moved toward a different kind of economy that led to increased production and increased income for farmers and other Chinese workers. China's gross domestic product (GDP), which is the broadest measure of a nation's production of goods and services, has quadrupled since 1978. In 2002, China's GDP reached $5.7 trillion, second only to the United States in the global economy. Of this total, about 15 percent ($855 billion) came from agriculture, 51 percent ($2.9 trillion) came from industry and construction, and nearly 34 percent ($1.9 trillion) came from other services.[1]

Mining and Power

Coal mining is another significant part of China's economy. Found throughout China, especially in the north, coal is China's leading source of energy. Coal-fired electric plants provide more than 70 percent of the nation's electricity. China also mines and exports iron ore, magnesium, mercury, and salt.

China is also increasingly turning to hydroelectric projects for power. The Gezhouba Dam includes two hydroelectric plants on the Yangzi River and a related project, the Three Gorges Dam, is under construction and expected to be completed in 2009.

To Market, to Market

As of 2001, industry employed the second-highest percentage of the Chinese workforce (22 percent), after agriculture. Most of China's industries are concentrated along the eastern coast. Steel, transportation, and construction are the dominant fields. Brick, tile, cement, and food-processing

▲ *Hangzhou, praised by Marco Polo as one of the most beautiful cities in the world, is known for its tea cultivation.*

plants are also common throughout China. Shanghai, a large city on the East China Sea, and Guangzhou, which is one of China's largest cities in the south, remain the country's main garment producers, but many new textile mills have been built in other fertile areas, where they can depend on locally grown cotton.

Years ago, Chinese manufacturers had the most success selling watches, jewelry, bicycles, and appliances such as sewing machines. Today, the Chinese manufacture and export a wide variety of products, including heavy machinery; textiles, clothing, and footwear; toys; electronics; and sports equipment. Twenty-two percent of China's exports go to the United States, and nearly 15 percent to Japan. Other major trading partners include South Korea, Taiwan, and Germany.

China became a member of the World Trade Organization in 2001, which has improved the nation's place in the global economy, but the Chinese government has been criticized for not following all WTO rules. There are concerns about China's Communist policies and questions about whether China should be allowed to have special trade status.

▷ Transport and Tourism

In the coming years, travel within China will become easier when a massive network of twelve major highways—five north-south routes and seven east-west—that will total nearly twenty-two thousand miles is completed. At the beginning of 2003, 75 percent of the highway network had been built, and 20 percent more was under construction. Once the project is completed (expected in 2008), more than two hundred cities will be connected by highways.

▲ *Barkhor Street in Lhasa, whose names translates as "the sacred place." The Qinghai-Tibet Railway, when completed, will reach Lhasa.*

The nation is also building the Qinghai-Tibet Railway, which, when completed, will feature the highest-elevation track in the world. The Guangdong-Hainan Railway, opened in January 2003, is a technological marvel. Two rail stations in the Guangdong and Hainan provinces are connected by a railroad built on a ferry, which shuttles train cars back and forth.

Tourism to China is becoming more popular as well. Most travelers to China come from Japan, Korea, Russia, and the United States, but Chinese authorities estimate that more than one million people from the United States visited China in the year 2000, when it was the fifth most-visited country in the world. The country is preparing for a huge tourist influx in 2008, when the Olympic Games are scheduled to be held in Beijing.

Confucius to Communism: History

According to Chinese legend, the first Chinese dynasty was formed around 2205 B.C. by a very wise king named Yu. Under Yu's leadership, the kings of the Xia dynasty were known for their wisdom and virtue. Yu is considered a cultural hero to the Chinese, who believe that he built canals to control floods. During the Xia period, the Chinese may have kept domestic animals, used bronze weapons, and rode in chariots.

Although the Xia dynasty may be mostly mythical, it is often considered the beginning of the Chinese dynasty system, which was the main governing system in China for thousands of years. A dynasty is usually run by a family group that can hold power for several generations. In China, dynasties were usually stripped of their power only through warfare and political disorder. Yet the determination of some dynasty leaders led to several important cultural developments.

▶ The Early Dynasties

Among China's many notable dynasties, the first true historic dynasty is the Shang, which ruled from about 1523 to 1027 B.C. During this period, Chinese society became more organized. People recorded important information by carving it onto bones or turtle shells—the beginnings of Chinese writing. These carvings included ancient vocabulary and dating systems, as well as information about harvest cycles and building locations.

The Shang dynasty was overthrown in 1027 B.C. by the Zhou dynasty, which lasted until 221 B.C. and ushered in a creative new period in Chinese history. The great Chinese philosopher Confucius (551 to 479 B.C.) lived during the part of this dynasty known as the Spring and Autumn period. During this period, the power of the Zhou kings became decentralized, and free thinking and technological advancements increased. Another philosopher living at nearly the same time, Lao Zi (Lao Tze), founded Taoism, which promoted a simple way of life in harmony with the natural world. Lao Zi's teachings were in sharp contrast to the warlike behavior and political takeovers common during the Warring States period,

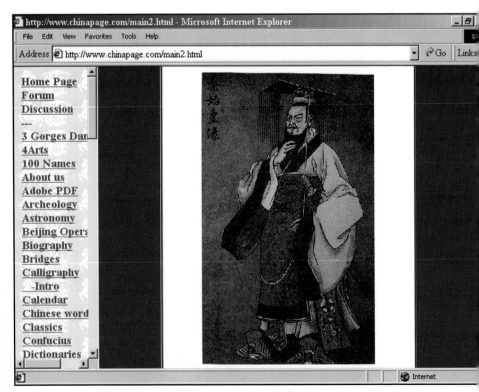

▲ Qin Shi Huangdi was the first emperor of the Qin dynasty, the dynasty that first unified China.

which followed the Spring and Autumn period. The Warring States period, which lasted from 475 to 221 B.C., was a time when massive wars divided the country.

When the Qin dynasty came to power around 221 B.C., it conquered the warring states and unified the country for the first time. To keep out tribes that might invade the country, Qin leaders ordered existing fortifications to be connected in what was the construction of the first Great Wall of China. Although the wall would be built and rebuilt over the following centuries, much of the initial construction took place during the Qin dynasty.

China in the Middle Ages

After the Qin and Han dynasties, there was a long period of war and disunity in China that lasted until the early years of the Tang dynasty (A.D. 618 to 907). But during that dynasty, China enjoyed several centuries of peaceful rule and creative development. For example, the Tang dynasty saw a blossoming of the arts, such as poetry, sculpture, and painting. Later, the Song dynasty (960 to 1279) was marked by improvements in printing and education. Novels were first written and read in China during this period.

While the Song dynasty ruled central China, numerous Mongol tribes were organizing in the north. Eventually, these tribes were unified by Genghis Khan (which translates as "great ruler"), who was feared and respected as a strong political and military leader. Genghis Khan's massive army conquered most of northern China, as well as portions of the Middle East and Eastern Europe. When he was killed in battle in 1227, these vast lands were divided among his sons and grandsons.

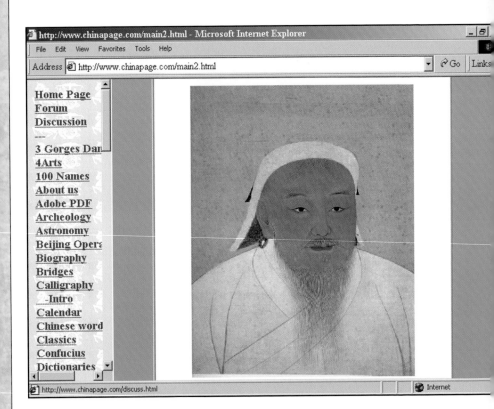

▲ *Mongol ruler Genghis Khan and his army conquered more than two thirds of the known world in the thirteenth century.*

One of these grandsons, Kublai Khan, would become famous as well. Kublai Khan founded the Yuan dynasty, which ruled China in the thirteenth and fourteenth centuries. During his reign, Kublai Khan ordered the rebuilding and extension of canals and highways. He encouraged religious tolerance and promoted education and trade. Several Europeans, including the Venetian traveler Marco Polo, visited China during this period. Marco Polo famously wrote about his visits to Asia, including the great capital city, now called Beijing, that was built by Kublai Khan.

Expansion and Change

As China moved toward modern times, the large nation continued to expand. During the Qing dynasty, which lasted from 1644 to 1911, China reached its greatest territorial expansion, including present-day Mongolia, Tibet, Nepal, and Turkistan. International commerce expanded as well. Over the next two centuries, however, China would come under growing pressure from outside nations over land and trade. The Qing would be China's last dynasty.

Foreign Trade

Beginning in the early eighteenth century, China had established a thriving trade with Great Britain, exchanging Chinese tea for British textiles and metal goods. Yet along with the growth in trade came an increase in opium smuggling. Opium is an addictive drug made from the poppy flower. As the value of Chinese tea rose in England, British merchants began smuggling opium into China to balance out trading, even though China had banned the import of opium. This led to the first of two Opium Wars between China and Great Britain and eventually other Western nations.

In 1839, China had tried to enforce its opium ban by destroying all the opium held by merchants in the port city of Guangzhou. Angry British responded by attacking several Chinese coastal cities. Defeated, Chinese authorities signed the Treaty of Nanjing and a later treaty that opened several coastal cities to trade with Britain. In addition, the city of Hong Kong was surrendered to Britain (which governed the city until 1997, when it was returned to Chinese control).

In the 1850s, a second Opium War erupted, this time with British and French troops attacking Chinese cities. China was forced to sign another agreement, the Treaty of Tianjin, which opened even more ports to foreign trade. This time, France, Russia, and the United States were party to the treaty, meaning they could trade with China as well.

▷ Growing Conflicts

As China was facing pressures from the Western world, it was also erupting internally. Beginning in 1850, a group of Chinese, including many from the poorer classes, led the Taiping Rebellion in an attempt to overthrow the Qing dynasty. Yet Britain and other Western nations were concerned that if the Qing dynasty was conquered, foreign trade might collapse as well. With Western military assistance, the Qing rulers were able to put down the rebellion.

But natural disasters and famine led many Chinese to immigrate to the United States—which they called the "Golden Mountain."

During the last half of the nineteenth century, foreign control over China

◁ *A Boxer, one of the militant Chinese who tried to rid China of foreigners and their influence in the early 1900s.*

continued to grow. Great Britain and the United States promoted the Open Door policy, which meant that all nations could enjoy equal access to trade with China. However, foreign countries still influenced different areas of China, dividing the country. From 1883 to 1885, China and France went to war over territory in Vietnam, which ended with France gaining that territory. By 1894, China found itself at war with Japan in the first Sino-Japanese War. The two countries fought for control of Korea, which had lived under Beijing's influence for years. Japan's more modern army easily defeated the Chinese military.

By the very end of the nineteenth century, the Chinese made a desperate attempt to block foreign control. In 1898, a secret Chinese society known as the Boxers began a movement against foreign influence and foreigners themselves that ended with a violent uprising in 1900. Eventually, an organized army of British, French, Japanese, Russian, German, and American troops held back the uprising. However, the Western nations and Japan agreed that China should be able to maintain some territorial power.

The End of Dynasties

In 1911, with the failure of domestic reforms, the Qing dynasty was overthrown by the Kuomintang, or Chinese Nationalist Party, led by Sun Yat-sen. A republic was formed with Sun Yat-sen the provisional leader of the government. But repressive controls soon followed, and by the end of World War I, a period of chaos marked by warlords seizing power ensued.

In 1921, two professors at Beijing University founded the Chinese Communist party, although in the beginning it attracted only a few members. Communism, a political system in which the national government controls the economy,

▲ This representation of Mao Zedong, the central figure of Chinese communism for more than forty years, shows him standing next to a flag on which the images of Stalin, Lenin, Engels, and Marx appear. All were leading figures in the history of socialism or communism.

with the idea that goods will be shared equally by all people, had already become the system of government in the former Soviet Union earlier in the twentieth century. In China, the Communist party would eventually become one of the most powerful Communist organizations in the world.

In 1927, a soldier and political leader named Chiang Kai-shek tried to purge his Nationalist party of Communists, leading to a period of conflict between the Chinese Communists and the Nationalists. Ten years later, as a second Sino-Japanese War broke out, the two parties continued to fight a civil war with each other, even as they both fought Japanese invaders during the Second World War. With the end of that war, in 1945, China was in a much-weakened state, and the feud between the Nationalists and the Communists continued. Years of war between China and Japan and between parties within China itself led to at least a passive acceptance of communism. On October 1, 1949, with the United States no longer supporting the Nationalist government of Chiang Kai-shek, the Communists, who held the capital at Beijing, proclaimed a central people's government. The Nationalist government was moved to the island of Taiwan in December of that year.

In 1949, Mao Zedong became chairman of the central government of the People's Republic of China, as the Communist-run nation was called. For many decades, Mao was the face of Chinese communism. As a reminder of this, a large portrait of Mao hangs in Tiananmen Square, the large public gathering place in Beijing. In an attempt to separate Chinese communism from Russian communism, Mao in 1958 launched an economic program known as the Great Leap Forward. The program, however, led to poverty and starvation for millions of Chinese people. In 1959, Liu Shaoqi, an opponent of the failed program, became chairman of the central government council, although Mao remained chairman of the Communist party politburo. Mao's attempts to reassert his ideology led to the Cultural Revolution of the 1960s and 1970s in which Mao and his wife, Jiang Qing, mobilized Chinese students to attack the views of Communist party officials, their teachers, and others considered "intellectuals." The Cultural Revolution lasted from 1966 to 1976, the year of Mao's death.

▲ *This poster captures the Red Guard's throwing away of old traditions during the Cultural Revolution of the 1960s and 1970s.*

▷ Dealing With Democracy

After Mao's death, his successors gradually loosened the government's tight control on the economy, introducing a market-based system that was more favorable to Western nations. In 1979, China set up formal diplomatic relations with the United States. Yet as economic controls were relaxed, the Communist party kept strong political controls. These included government restrictions on where people in China could travel and even how many children each family could have.

In June 1989, Chinese students staged a large rally in Tiananmen Square, demonstrating their support for democracy. Others soon joined the protest, until more than one million people filled the square. On the nights of June 3 and 4, however, Chinese leaders used force to end the demonstration, killing hundreds of protesters.

Since the Tiananmen Square massacre, China's relationship with the Western world, and especially the United States, has been tense. In May 1999, the Chinese embassy in Belgrade, Serbia, was accidentally bombed by forces of the North Atlantic Treaty Organization (NATO), an alliance of European nations and the United States and Canada that was originally formed in 1949 to combat Russian aggression during the cold war period. The bombing, though a mistake, set off anti-American demonstrations in Beijing. In April 2001, a Chinese fighter jet and a U.S. surveillance plane collided in mid-air, killing the Chinese pilot. However, the United States still signed a trade agreement that paved the way for China's entry into the World Trade Organization in 2001.

China's future may be looking up—literally. In October 2003, China became only the third nation, after the United States and Russia, to launch a manned space mission. The *Shenzhou 5* spacecraft carried "taikonaut" Yang Liwei, a lieutenant colonel and former fighter pilot in the Chinese Air Force, into orbit for about twenty-one hours.[1] Coming at a time when both the United States and Russia have suffered setbacks in their space programs, China's manned launch into space was hailed within the country as a great political and technological victory.

Chapter 6 ▶

The "Golden Mountain": Chinese Americans

As Chinese immigration to the United States began in earnest in the mid-nineteenth century, the American government was dealing with sectional conflicts that eventually erupted into the American Civil War (1861–65). After the war, the federal government wanted to unite the country, in more ways than one. In 1862, a route was chosen for a transcontinental railroad. Two companies managed the railroad construction: the Central Pacific, building from the West, and the Union Pacific, building from the East. In addition to using Civil War veterans, both companies employed thousands of immigrants to build the railroads. The Central Pacific hired as many as ten thousand Chinese, who suffered many hardships, including discrimination. For example, Chinese workers were paid less than non-Chinese workers. During the winter of 1865–66, nearly twelve hundred Chinese immigrants died from accidents, avalanches, and explosions while working on the railroad.

Once the transcontinental railroad was completed in 1869, Chinese immigrants were hired to work on railroad projects in other parts of the country. As Chinese immigrants dispersed, other businesses were established as well, and the Chinese in America often worked in laundries or restaurants or entered the fishing and shrimp industries.

▷ More Discrimination

By the late 1870s, non-Asian workers' groups in the United States were growing resentful of the Chinese, with whom they competed for jobs. Violence against Chinese, especially in California, began to rise. Citizens called for the passage of laws banning or controlling Chinese immigration. The United States Congress eventually passed the Chinese Exclusion Act of 1882, which barred the entry of Chinese laborers into the United States for a period of ten years. A second Exclusion Act two years later was even stricter, although Chinese immigrants could still enter the country. To do so, they had to prove that they were students, tourists, ministers, or performed other types of jobs that were not considered threats to American workers.

Several American groups felt that even these exemptions were too lenient. They wanted to slam the door shut on the Chinese, even though European immigrants were still allowed to enter the country. The Geary Act of 1892 barred nearly all Chinese from immigrating to the United States. The Chinese who already lived in the United States were required to carry a residence certificate at all times, or they risked being deported, or made to leave the country. But as difficult as these measures made life for the Chinese in America, they were remarkably resilient people, who managed to carve out lives for themselves and their families.

Angel Island

To enforce these immigration laws, the federal government built an immigration station on Angel Island, in San Francisco Bay. Like Ellis Island in New York Harbor, which accepted immigrants from Europe, Angel Island was one of the first entry points for Asian immigrants. During its heyday from 1910 to 1940, the Angel Island station processed about 250,000 Chinese immigrants. American officials hoped to deport most Chinese, who were detained at Angel Island for weeks or months, and sometimes even years.

▲ *The immigration center at Angel Island in San Francisco was an entry point to America for many Asians, including Chinese. It was also, however, a place where Asian immigrants were held and some deported.*

The barracks were like a prison. Frustrated and bored, Chinese detainees sometimes wrote poems or messages on the barrack walls, some of which can still be seen today.

As the nation entered World War II, in which China was an ally of the United States, the federal government relaxed its views toward the Chinese. When Madame Chiang Kai-shek toured America in 1943, many citizens were impressed. That same year, the government finally reversed the Exclusion Acts, allowing Chinese immigrants to become American citizens.

▷ The Growth of Chinatowns

Despite the American government's efforts to limit immigration, Chinese immigrants continued to form communities in major cities across the United States. In large cities, they formed what became known as "Chinatowns," in which Chinese Americans started their own businesses. As places where Chinese Americans could still have traditional food, speak their native language, and congregate with other

Chinese, Chinatowns served to remind immigrants of their homeland.

The first Chinatown was created in San Francisco in the late nineteenth century. After a large earthquake and fire in 1906 leveled most of the city, officials rebuilt Chinatown with Chinese-style architecture and attractions, hoping to boost tourism to the city. Today, San Francisco's Chinatown is a thriving community that abounds with cultural activities.

East to New York

In the nineteenth century, as discrimination increased on the West Coast, many Chinese immigrants moved east to New York City. This trend continued into the twentieth century. Today the growth of New York's Chinatown has outpaced San Francisco's Chinatown. With about a quarter of a million Chinese Americans living in the borough of Manhattan, and thousands more living in the nearby boroughs of Queens and Brooklyn, New York has the

▲ *The history of one family's life as Chinese in America can be seen in this family portrait, which features a collage of ancestors.*

largest concentration of Chinese people outside of Southeast Asia.

New York's Chinatown is crowded with restaurants offering traditional food and newsstands that sell newspapers printed in Chinese. Many new Chinese immigrants work in restaurants or garment factories. Despite working long hours and often making little money, many Chinese immigrants still see America as the "Golden Mountain" of hope and promise. Zan Ng, for example, immigrated to New York in 1975, landing a job washing dishes. After learning English, however, he eventually became the owner of several successful businesses. "How did I make it here? Hard work, saving, and keeping any eye out for opportunity," Ng told a reporter. "That's how you do it."[1]

Ethnic Pride

In addition to being a gathering place for Chinese immigrants, Chinatowns are valued as a way for Chinese Americans to hold on to Chinese history and culture. In New York City, for example, middle-class Chinese Americans—known as ABCs (American-Born Chinese)—often bring their children from the suburbs to visit Chinatown where they might take Chinese language classes or practice traditional customs.

They also might simply enjoy the food that is part of their heritage and has become one of the most popular cuisines in the United States and other Western nations. Chinese immigrants and Chinese Americans operate restaurants in most cities and large towns. These restaurants often specialize in the cuisine of a particular region in China, since Chinese cuisine is so varied.

Chinese Americans have risen to fame in almost every field of work. Millions of less-famous Chinese Americans are putting their stamp on American society in their own ways, every day. Whatever they do, Chinese Americans often have a strong attachment to what was once their homeland. In a famous Chinese poem that is beloved by many who have settled outside China, the poem's narrator is awakened by bright moonlight. "Lowering my head," the narrator says afterwards, "I dream that I am home."[2]

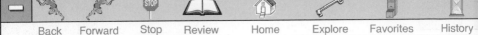

China Facts

1. The *World Factbook 2003*, "China," July 2003 estimated population,<www.cia.gov/cia/publications/factbook/geos/ch.html> (November 17, 2003).

2. Borgna Brunner, ed., *Time Almanac 2003* (Boston: Information Please, 2003), p. 748.

Chapter 1. An Ancient Heritage

1. Governor Gary Locke, Speech before the Indochina Chinese Refugee Association of Washington, February 8, 2003, <www.governor.wa.gov/speeches/speeches.asp> (October 4, 2003).

Chapter 2. A Staircase With Three Steps: Land and Climate

1. Borgna Brunner, ed. *Time Almanac 2003* (Boston: Information Please, 2002), p. 749.

Chapter 3. Yin and Yang: Culture

1. Amy Tan, *The Joy Luck Club* (New York: Random House, 1989), p. 288.

Chapter 4. Embracing the Future: Economy

1. The *World Factbook 2003*, "China: Economy," August 1, 2003,<http://www.cia.gov/cia/publications/factbook/geos/ch.html#Econ> (December 23, 2003).

Chapter 5. Confucius to Communism: History

1. Jim Yardley, "After 21 Hours, Chinese Spacecraft Land Safely," The *New York Times*, October 16, 2003.

Chapter 6. The "Golden Mountain": Chinese Americans

1. Joel L. Swerdlow, "New York's Chinatown," *National Geographic*, August 1998, p. 63.

2. Lynn Pan, *Sons of the Yellow Emperor: A History of the Chinese Diaspora* (Tokyo: Kodansha International, 1994), p. 21.

Further Reading

Baldwin, Robert F. *Daily Life in Ancient and Modern Beijing.* Minneapolis: Runestone Press, 1999.

Barth, Kelly, ed. *The Tiananmen Square Massacre.* San Diego: Greenhaven Press/Thomson Gale, 2003.

Chen, Da. *China's Son: Growing Up in the Cultural Revolution.* New York: Delacorte Press, 2001.

Cotterell, Arthur. *Ancient China.* New York: Knopf, 1994.

Faulkner, Anne. *Mao Zedong: From Farmer's Son to Communist Leader.* Austin, Tex.: Raintree Steck-Vaughn Publishers, 2003.

Freedman, Russell. *Confucius: The Golden Rule.* New York: Arthur A. Levine Books, 2002.

Immell, Myra. *The Han Dynasty.* San Diego: Lucent Books, 2003.

Kizilos, Peter. *Tibet: Disputed Land.* Minneapolis: Lerner Publications, 2000.

O'Connor, Jane. *The Emperor's Silent Army: Terracotta Warriors of Ancient China.* New York: Viking, 2002.

Whiteford, Gary T. *China.* Philadelphia: Chelsea House Publishers, 2003.

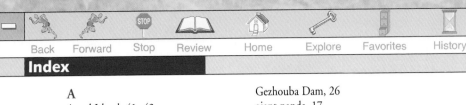
A

Angel Island, 41–42
area, 14
art, 21–23, 31

B

Beijing, 10–11, 16–17, 19, 28, 32, 35, 37, 39
Boxers, 34–35

C

Chiang Kai-shek, 36–37
Chinatowns, 42–45
Chinese Exclusion Act of 1882, 41–42
climate, 15
communism, 18–19, 27, 35–38
Confucianism, 20–21, 30
Cultural Revolution, 19, 37

D

dynasties, 29–35

E

economy
    agriculture, 25–26
    construction, 25–26
    manufacturing, 26–27
    mining, 26
    steel, 26
    tourism, 10, 12, 28
    transportation, 15–17, 26–28
education, 19, 31

F

famous Chinese Americans, 12–13, 24
festivals, 21
foreign trade, 33–35

G

games, 23–24
Geary Act of 1892, 41
geography
    East China Sea, 16, 27
    Himalaya Mountains, 15, 18
    Kunlun Mountains, 18
    Mount Everest, 15
    South China Sea, 16
    Yangzi River, 15, 17, 26
    Yellow Mountains, 12
    Yellow River, 15
    Yellow Sea, 16
Genghis Khan, 31–32

Gezhouba Dam, 26
giant panda, 17
Grand Canal, 15–16
Great Wall of China, 10, 31
Guangdong-Hainan Railway, 28
Guangzhou, 27, 33

H

Hong Kong, 10, 17, 33
hydroelectric power, 26

K

Kublai Khan, 32

L

literature, 21–22, 31

M

Mao Zedong, 11, 19, 36–38

N

Nationalist party, 18, 36–37

O

Opium Wars, 33–34

P

Palace Museum, 11, 16
Polo, Marco, 32
population, 10

R

religion, 18, 20

S

Shanghai, 10, 17, 19, 27
Sino-Japanese Wars, 35–36
space program, 39
sports, 23

T

Taiwan, 17–18, 37
Taoism, 21, 30
terra-cotta warriors and horses, 11–12
Three Gorges Dam, 26
Tiananmen Square, 11–12, 17, 38–39
Tibet, 15, 18, 33
transcontinental railroad, 40

W

World Trade Organization, 27, 39

Y

"yin and yang," 19